# Calligraphy Copybook

_____

_____

Life Style Daily
All rights are reserved. 2022
No part of this publication may be reproduced, stored in a retrieval system or transmitted in any form or by any means, electronic, mechanical, photocopying, recording or otherwise, without prior permission.

A place for the inkblot,

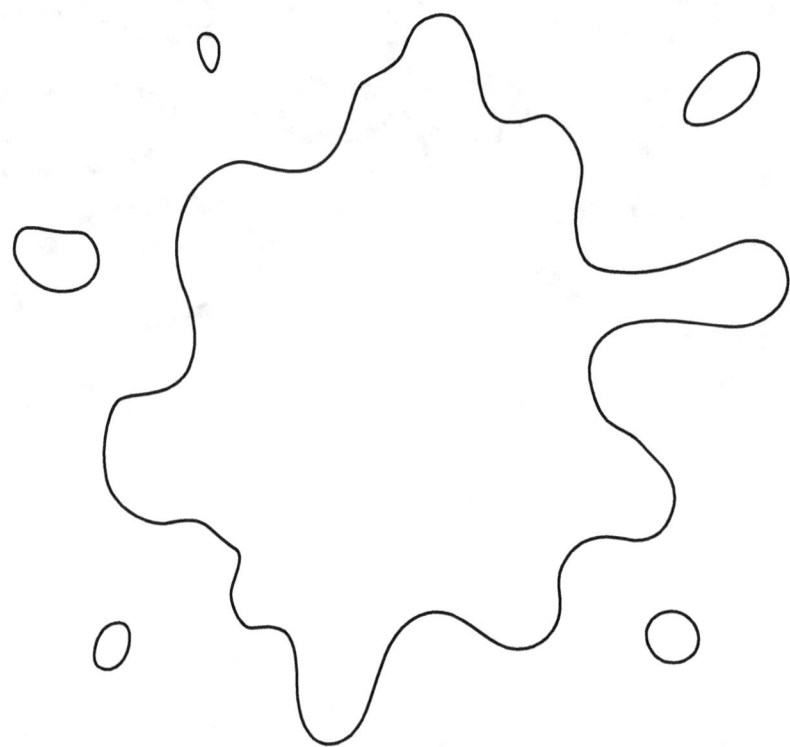

If you're going to learn to letter, we've got to get through a bit of vocabulary words first so don't start skipping pages just yet!

DOWNSTROKE: Any movement downward with the writing instrument. These lines are thick!

UPSTROKE: Any movement upward with the writing instrument.

ASCENDER: The part of the letter that extends above the mean line.

DESCENDER: The part of the letter that falls below the baseline.

FLOURISH: These are the added strokes and swashes used to decorate or enhance letters.

CROSSBAR: Horizontal strokes on letters such as 't', 'f', and uppercase 'H'.

LETTERFORM: The form or shape of a letter.

A place for the inkblot,

# Important Tips

One: The most important tip is to write slowly! Think of lettering as drawing each letter, instead of just writing each letter.

Two: Start with a pencil. You can draw and erase as you fine-tune your letters!

Three: Pick up your pen in between strokes. Unlike cursive where your pen flows on the paper through the entire word, lettering is made up of multiple strokes.

Four: As mentioned, in calligraphy down strokes are always thicker.

Five: Upstrokes are always thinner.

Six: Practice! Master your letterforms first! Then master connecting those letters as you write full words. Once you have mastered connections, practice your composition and design!

In the next section, we will begin to draw our basic strokes & letterforms! Get those pencils, pens, and brush pens ready! Your lettering journey begins!

*Let's do this!*

*A place for the inkblot,*

| A | a | a | a | a | a | a | a |

A A A A A A A A

a a a a a a a a

B B B B B B B B

b b b b b b b b

C C C C C C C C

c c c c c c c c

D D D D D D D D

d d d d d d d d

E E E E E E E E

*A place for the inkblot,*

e e e e e e e e e e e

F F F F F F F

f f f f f f f

G G G G G G G

g g g g g g

H H H H H

h h h h h h h

J J J J J J J

i i i i i i i i i i i i i i i i

*A place for the inkblot,*

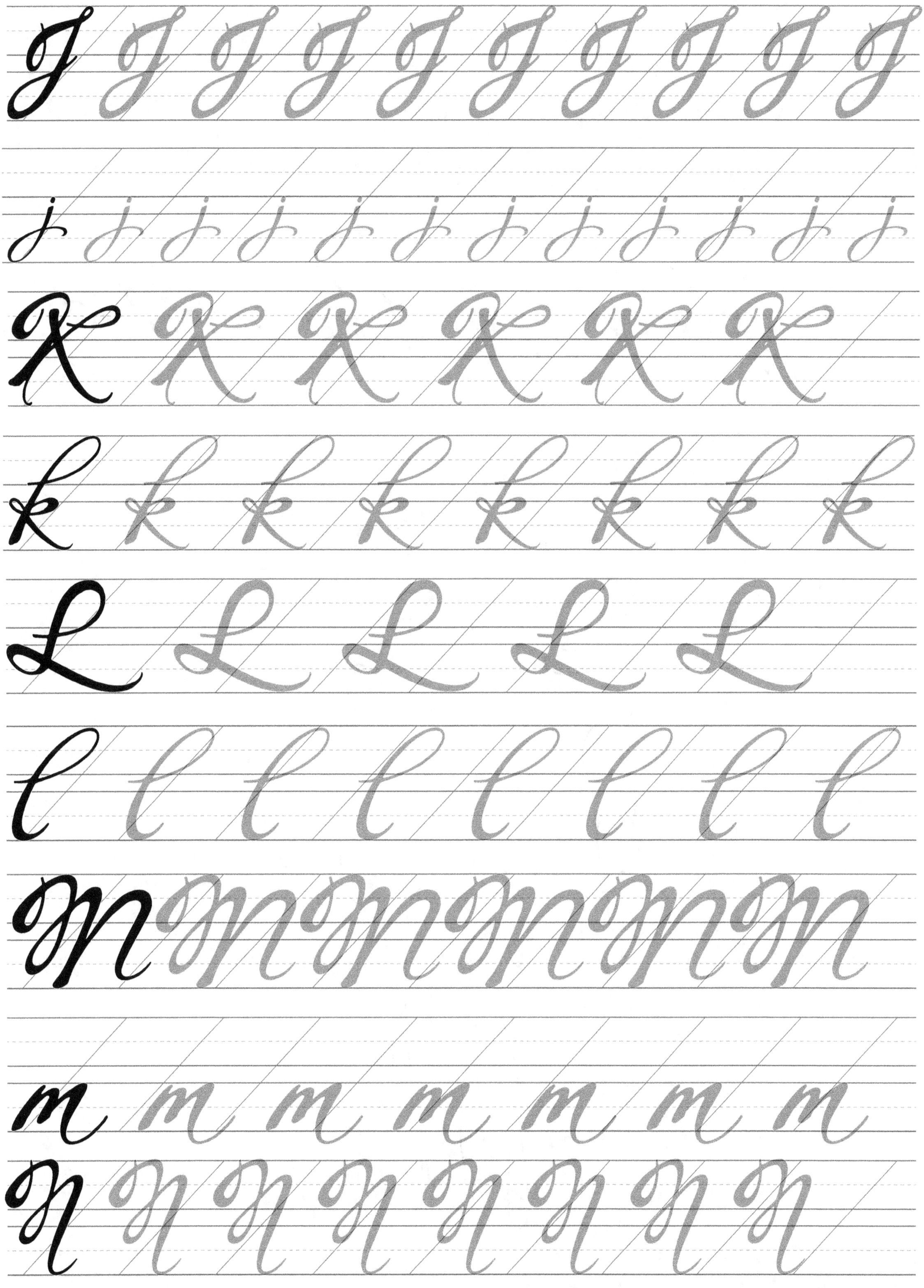
J J J J J J J J J J J
j j j j j j j j j j j j
K K K K K K
k k k k k k k k
L L L L L
l l l l l l l l
M M M M M M
m m m m m m m
N N N N N N N N

A place for the inkblot,

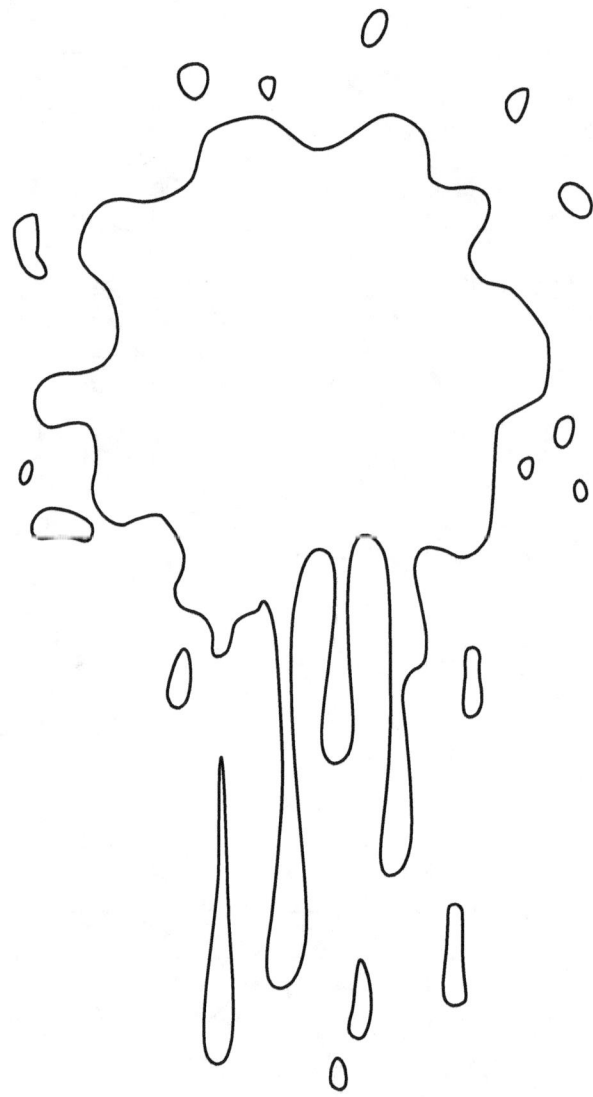

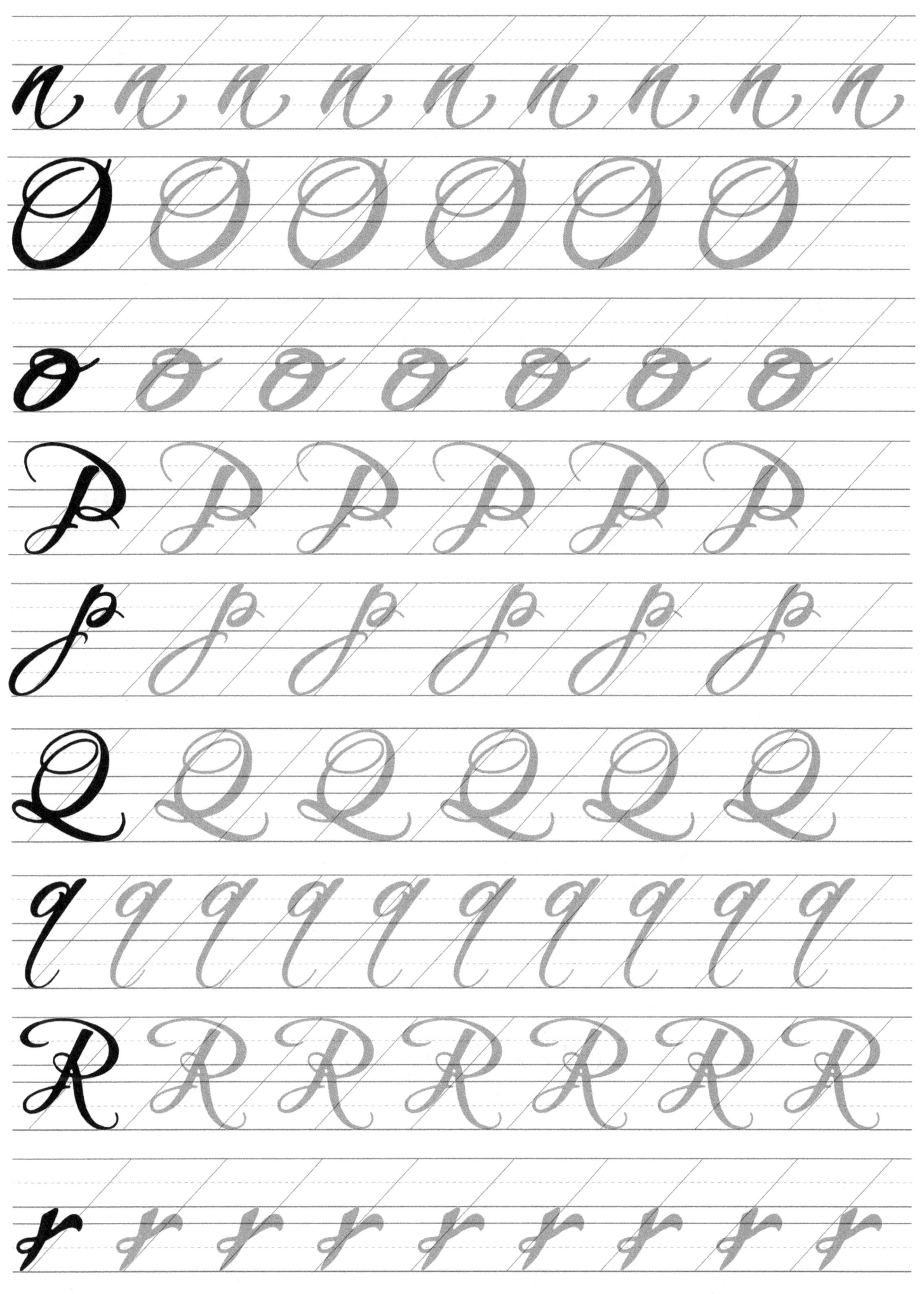

*A place for the inkblot,*

S S S S S S

s s s s s s s s s

T T T T T

t t t t t t t t t t t

U U U U U U U

u u u u u u u

V V V V V

v v v v v v v

W W W W W

# A place for the inkblot,

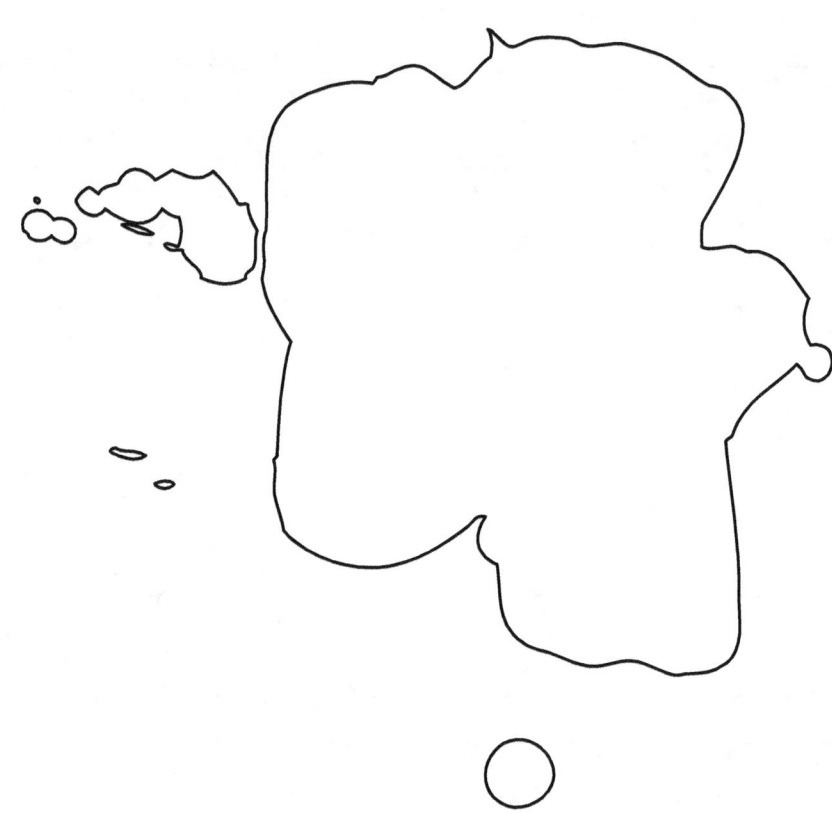

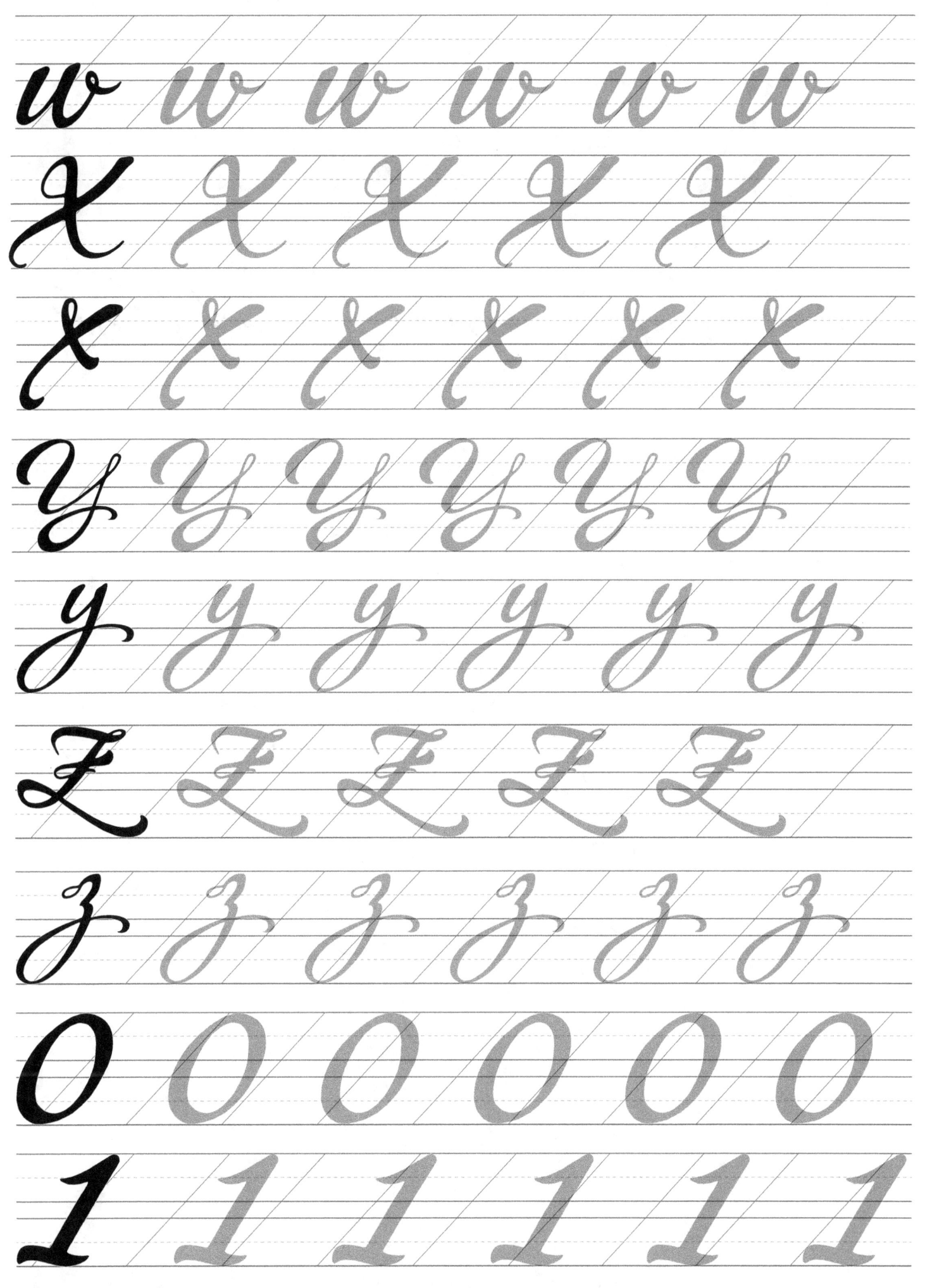

*A place for the inkblot,*

A place for the inkblot,

# Day 01

Is your birthright? You are not lacking; you are not too much; you are already simple enough, just as you are now in every minute. Trace the lettering. It doesn't have to be perfect. And that's okay. Allow yourself to focus on the process and maybe even let a smile creep up on your face. Enjoy the process. It's about the journey, and not the destination, remember?

*I am Already Enough*

*I am Already Enough*

*A place for the inkblot,*

A place for the inkblot,

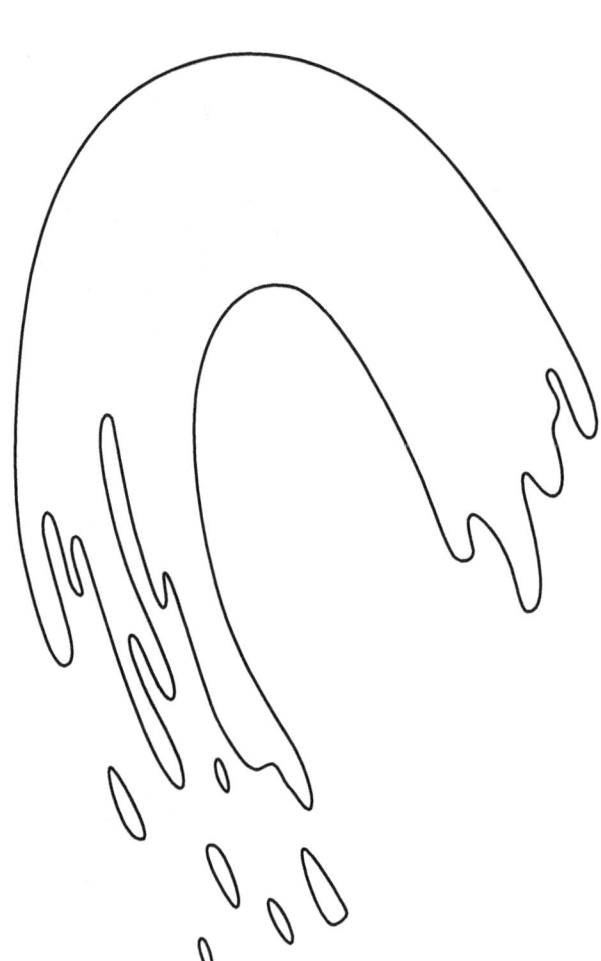

# 30 Days Of Affirmation

## Day 02

At this moment, you are infinitely supported by God, the Universe, a higher power, or whatever you believe. However, there is something deeper at work here than meets the eye, and it has your best interests at heart.

*I am infinitely supported*

*I am infinitely supported*

A place for the inkblot,

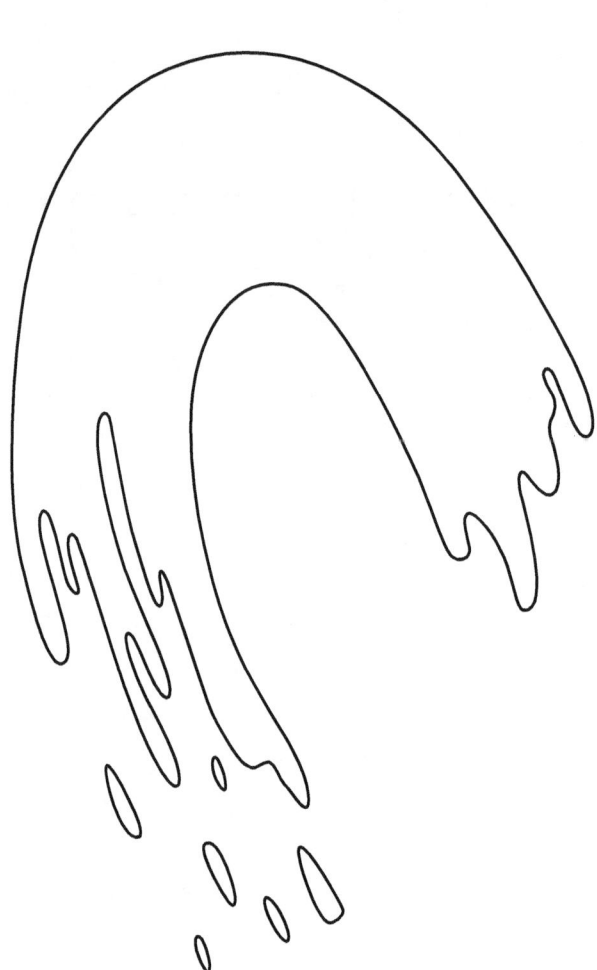

A place for the inkblot,

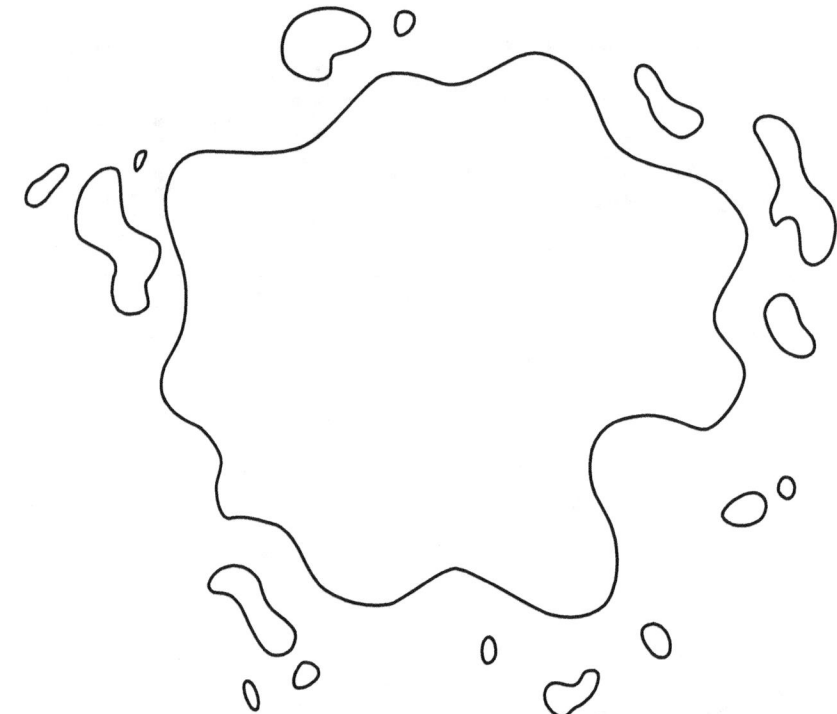

# Day 03

Have you ever had something good happen to you and realized that you're just waiting for the other shoe to drop? Like you know something bad is going to happen? Stop it. That's not necessarily true. Give yourself permission to allow good things to happen and expect that to continue as a pattern in your life.

*The better it gets the better it gets*

*A place for the inkblot,*

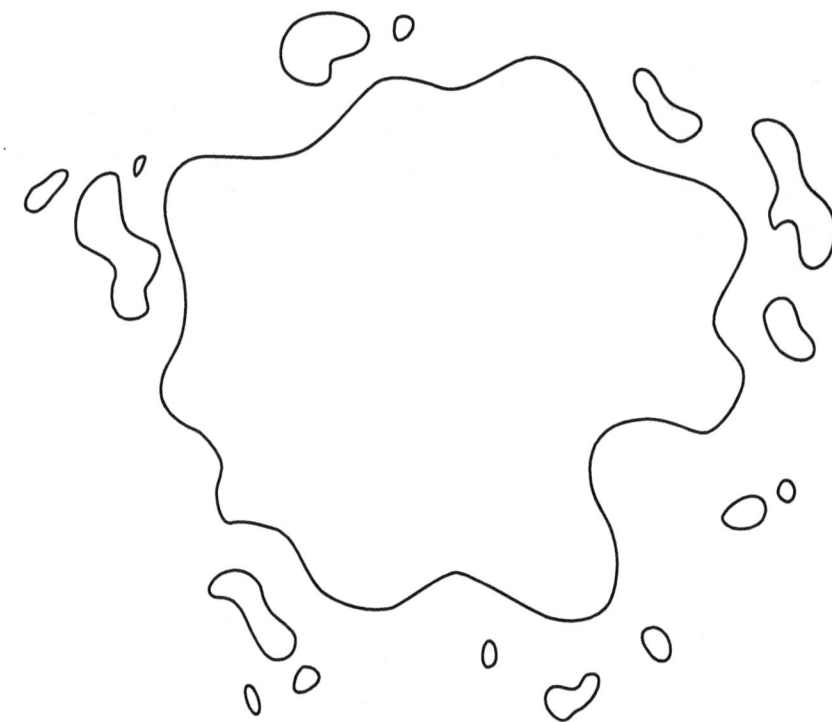

A place for the inkblot,

# 30 Days Of Affirmation

## Day 04

You haven't peaked yet and whether you are in a peak or a valley right now in your life, know that the best is yet to come. There are good days ahead, and looking forward to that is okay. This is a time to dream of all the outrageous things you only admit to yourself in the shower. The best is yet to come.

*The best is yet to come*

*The best is yet to come*

*A place for the inkblot,*

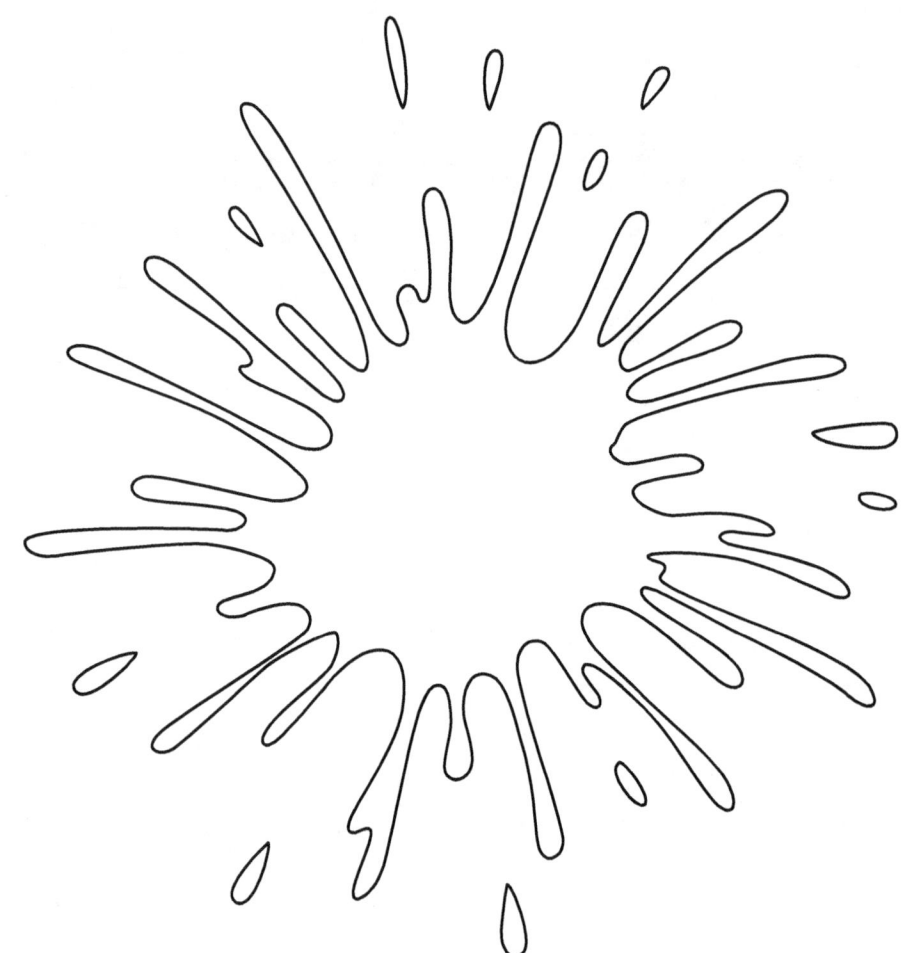

A place for the inkblot,

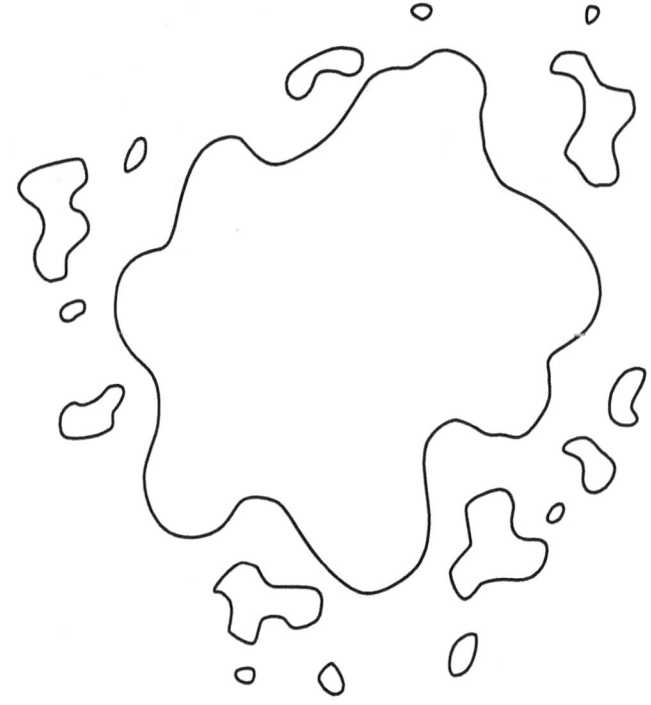

# 30 Days Of Affirmation

## Day 05

It is one of my favorite mantras. Find a penny on the street? More, please. Get an award at work? More, please. Sign a new client in your business? More, please! If you let it, these two simple words can transform your life.

*More please*

*More please More please*

A place for the inkblot,

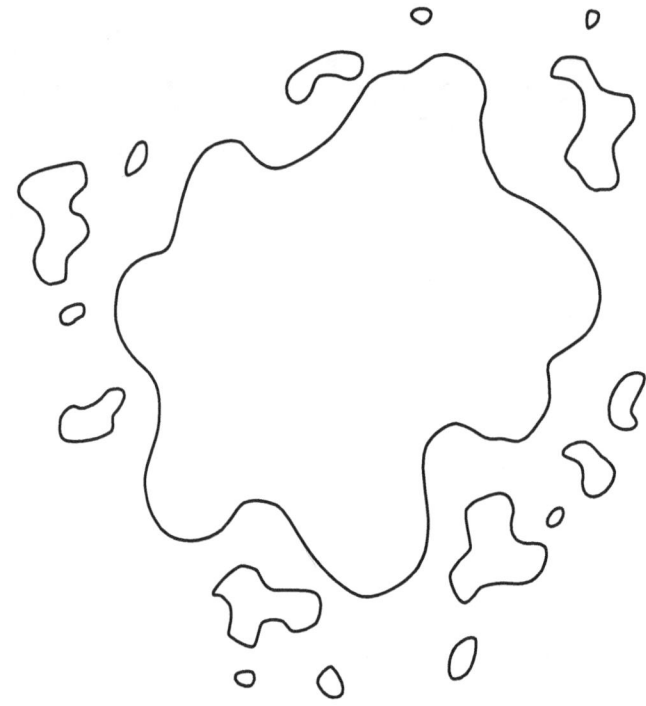

A place for the inkblot,

# 30 Days Of Affirmation

### Day 06

Just because you have had trials, tragedies, and low points in the past doesn't necessarily mean that you will have that in your future. Conversely, just because you've always succeeded in the past doesn't necessarily mean you will continue that path. Every moment, every second is an opportunity for something new. Your life is what you make of it, and your past does not equal your future.

*My past does not equal my future*

*A place for the inkblot;*

*A place for the inkblot,*

# 30 Days Of Affirmation

## Day 07

Have you ever played a game where you're throwing a ball back and forth, and you're like, "don't hit the tree, don't hit the tree?" Then you immediately hit the tree? That's because you focused on what you didn't want instead of what you did. Try focusing on what it is you want to call into your life. Instead of not getting fired, maybe it's keeping your job. Or better yet, getting a promotion. Instead of having just enough financially to get by, maybe focus on having extra left every month to invest. Focus on the result and not the process. That's some magic stuff right there.

*Where my attention goes, energy flows*

*A place for the inkblot,*

A place for the inkblot,

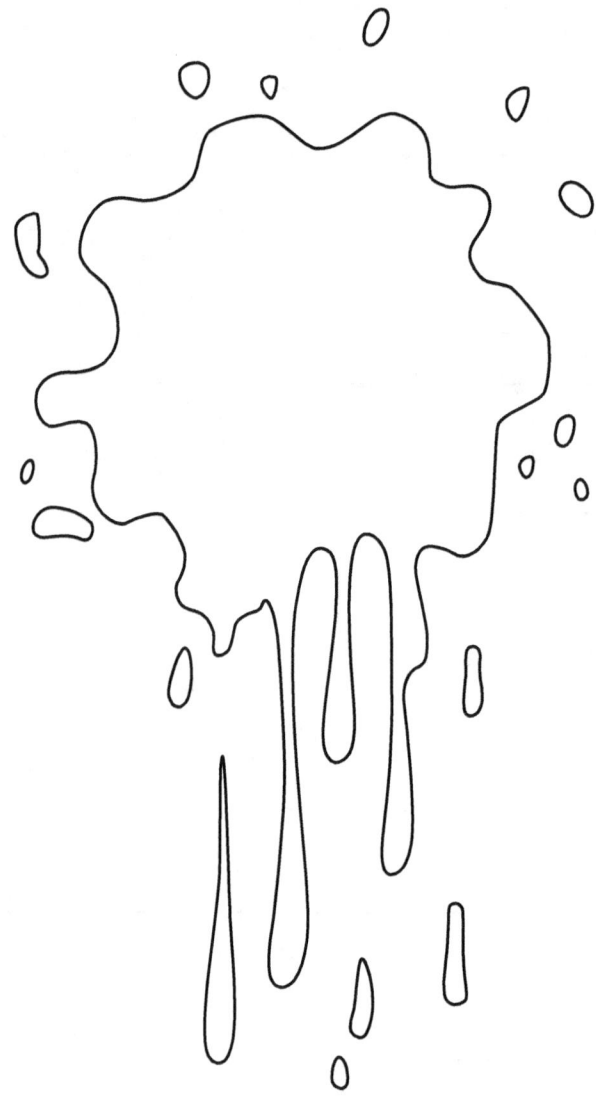

# 30 Days Of Affirmation
## Day 08

Trusting is a choice. After my son died, this was one of the hardest things for me, and it's a total lie to say I've mastered it. I come at this anew every day because choosing to trust is a frame of mind. While good things don't always happen to me, I know in my heart that somehow good can come from every situation. Even the terrible ones. I challenge you to try this one out and just see how it fits you in your life. Choose to trust.

*I choose to trust*

*I choose to trust*

A place for the inkblot,

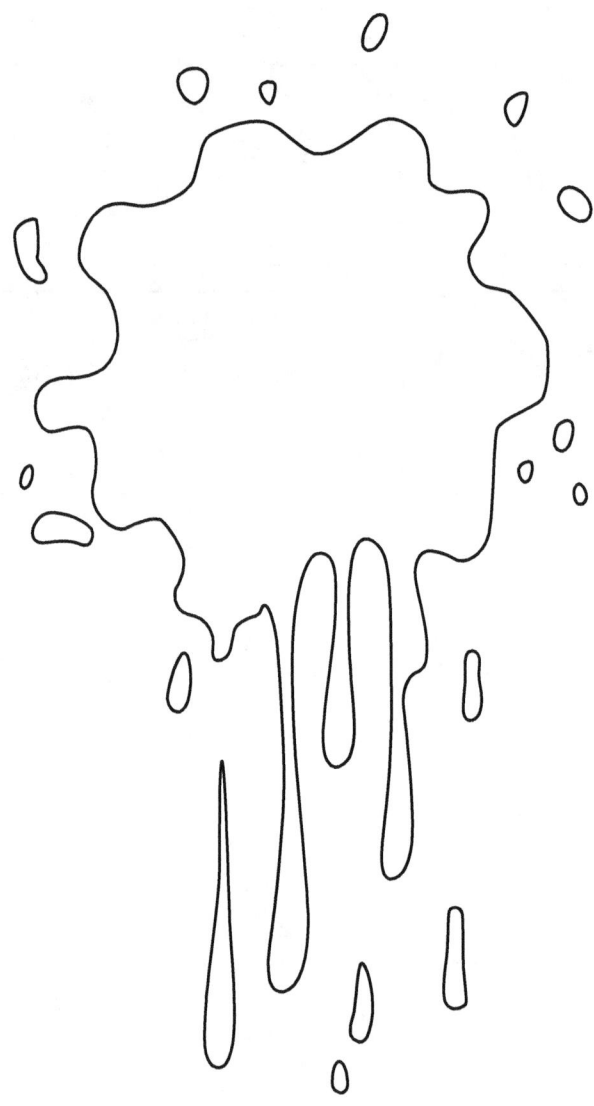

A place for the inkblot,

# 30 Days Of Affirmation

## Day 09

It is one of those mantras that can get exciting. All we have in life are the meanings and stories we give situations. It is a really fun belief to cultivate. Running late for school drop-off? Consider if you were guided and missed being in a car accident. Didn't you get that dream job? That wasn't your job; a better one is on its way. God's delays are not God's denials and if you have the attitude that things are always working out for you, watch how magnificent the blessings unfold in your life.

*Things are always working out for me*

*A place for the inkblot,*

*A place for the inkblot,*

# 30 Days Of Affirmation

## Day 10

Is this old school from the book The Secret by Rhonda Byrnes? Did you read that? The origins are even older from a book written at the turn of the last century by a man named Wallace Waddles, and exhaustive case studies prove this point. I am leaving it here, so you know that what is put in your heart is meant for you. If you have a big dream, it was put there for a reason. If you aren't sure what your plan is, that's okay too. See yourself happy and healthy and whole. Good things are on the way.

*Thoughts are things*

*Thoughts are things*

*A place for the inkblot,*

A place for the inkblot,

# Day 11

These are my personal mantra for the last ten years, and I've had a sign stating this hanging on my wall for at least that long. I sat with my kids when they were still little and tried to show them by example that we could do hard things. Sometimes it's something huge like climbing Mt Everest. Sometimes it's something that is a personal mountain that you're climbing. Remember, you have survived 100% of the things and situations you thought might kill you up until now. All evidence points that you will continue that pattern and stay these things too. You can do hard things.

*I can do hard things*

*I can do hard things*

A place for the inkblot,

*A place for the inkblot,*

# 30 Days Of Affirmation

## Day 12

Yes, you do! Trust that the tools, the people, and the resources you need are already on their way to you. Whatever needs to be done, if anything, you have the skills and grace to complete. You got this!

*I've got this*

*I've got this*

*A place for the inkblot,*

*A place for the inkblot,*

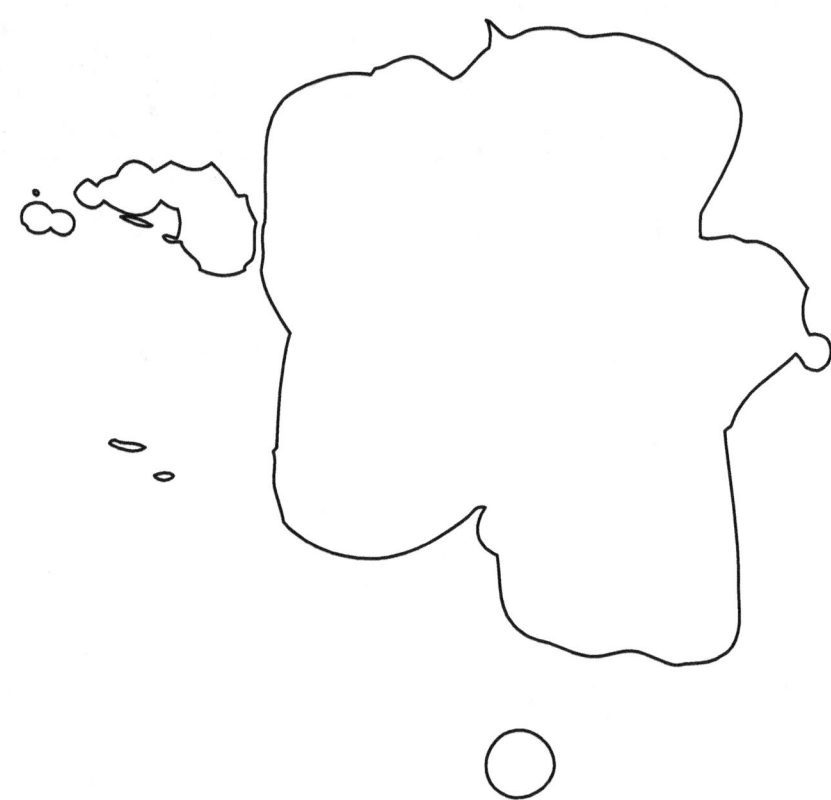

# 30 Days Of Affirmation

## Day 13

We're almost two weeks in, and if you haven't figured this out yet, a whole lot of this these affirmations are based on trust and choice. If you've had hard things happen in your life up until this point, it can be easy to throw your hands up in the air and proclaim that the deck is stacked against you. That God or Universe would allow something like this to happen. I know for sure I've asked that question over and over again personally. So this is a great place to jump in. Could you just create an experiment in your life? What if you are divinely guided and protected in all that you do? How would that change how you move through your life daily? Just try it out. Release attachment to the outcome and just think of it as an experiment. What would you do if you knew you could not fail?

*I am divinely guided and protected*

*A place for the inkblot,*

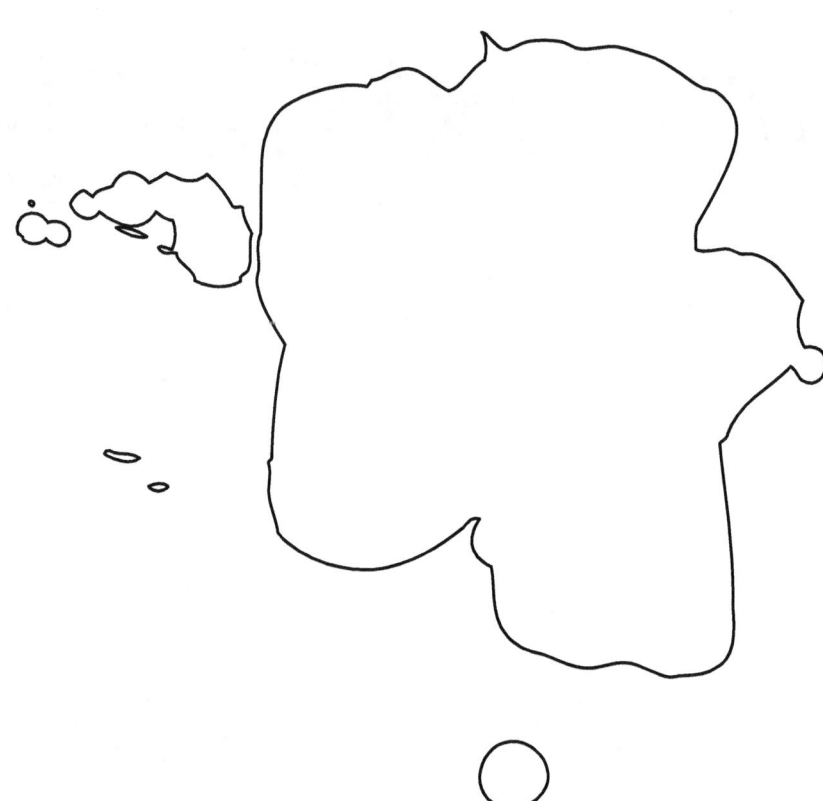

A place for the inkblot,

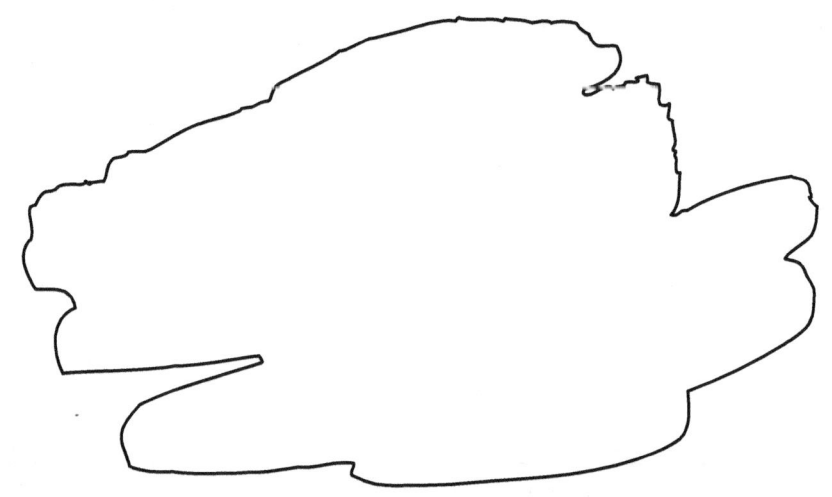

# 30 Days Of Affirmation

## Day 14

People sometimes say things to me like "gratitude is so basic" or "I can't be grateful you don't know what's happened to me." That's true, I don't know what's happened to you, but I guarantee you this: there is something you can be grateful for right now. Maybe it's your family, or perhaps it's that you live far away from your family. Perhaps the sun is shining, or maybe it's that you know the sun is there even if you can't see it right now. There is someone on the planet right now who would love to have your fingers, your toes, your limbs. So I'm going to let you in on a really big secret—you can't be angry or fearful AND grateful simultaneously. The solution to fear-based thoughts is gratitude.

*I am grateful*

*I am grateful*

*A place for the inkblot,*

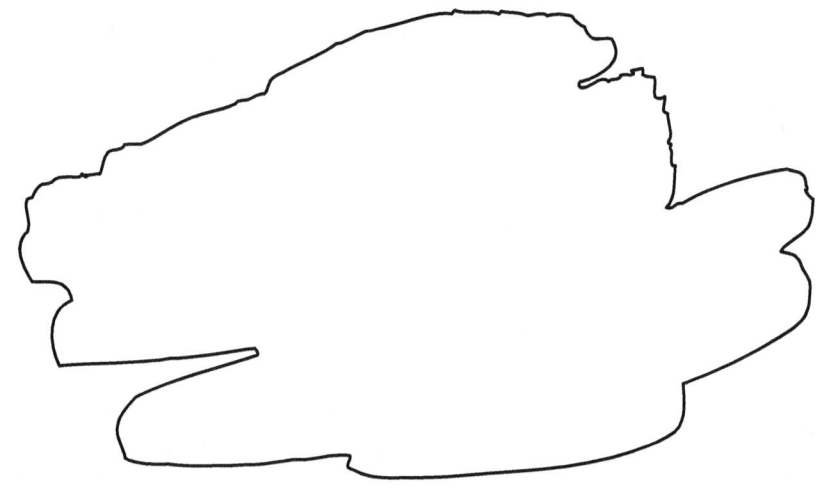

*A place for the inkblot,*

# 30 Days Of Affirmation

## Day 15

Feeling and believing that you are blessed is an attitude. It's the same as the people who think they're lucky. Are they lucky because they really are, or simply because they believe it? Guess what? Even the bad things that have happened to you led you somewhere good. I know like I know that to be true. Losing a child is one of the worst things one can go through. It was terrible. Somehow though, I'm still talking to you about being blessed. Is one of those, if I can do it-so can you things. If you don't have a happy ending, you're not at the end yet. Keep moving forward. You are blessed.

*A place for the inkblot,*

*A place for the inkblot,*

# 30 Days Of Affirmation

## Day 16

This is one of my favorite things to reflect on. Whether you are religious or spiritual, or agnostic, here's the truth. The odds of you being born on the day you were, to your parents, in the country you were born in, on this giant rock hurling through time and space at roughly 1,000 miles per hour are astronomically low. 1 in 400 trillion low. You are a gosh-darn real-life miracle. Cheers to you!

*I am a miracle*

*I am a miracle*

*A place for the inkblot,*

*A place for the inkblot,*

# 30 Days Of Affirmation
## Day 17

Being present isn't something that comes naturally to me. I love lists and doing things, and as a child, I was labeled as a real A-type personality. I remember when my kids were little, they would ask to play with me on the floor, and I remember thinking to myself, why? Don't worry, I still played with my kids, but I share that to illustrate that it can be really easy to keep looking ahead. Setting new goals and new ideas and new vacations and getting stuck in the day-to-day busyness of life. Covid was good at slowing many of us down, but if you go one step further and be in the moment, even for small amounts of time, it can be a serious game changer for you. Be present and watch your relationships grow and deepen, your work improves, and your love expands.

*I am present,*
*I am present*

*A place for the inkblot,*

A place for the inkblot,

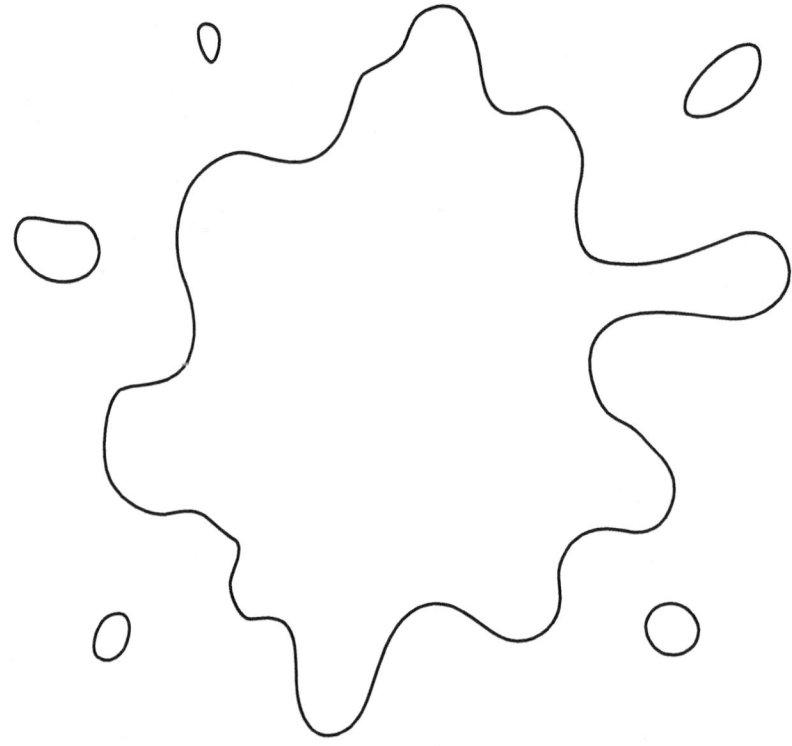

# 30 Days Of Affirmation

## Day 18

Oh yes, you do, honey! You can say this on repeat whether it's the 100th time today that you've been asked for a snack or you have a gigantic presentation to give in front of the board at work. It's so versatile and works for everyone in nearly every situation. You got this!

*I got this*

*I got this*

A place for the inkblot,

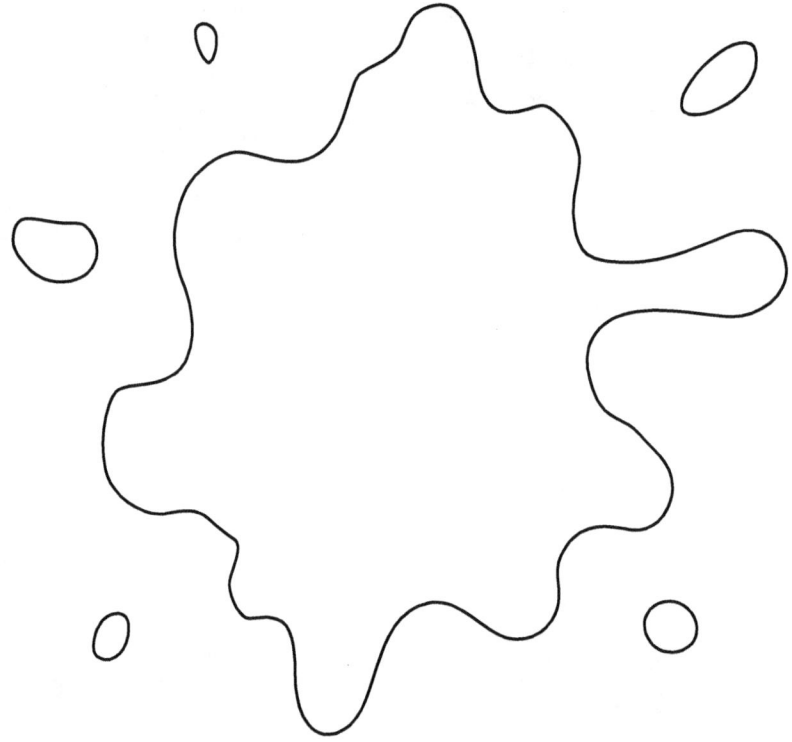

A place for the inkblot,

# 30 Days Of Affirmation

## Day 19

Today is a new day and a new opportunity. It was hard to get behind some of the lowest points in my life because it felt like a lie. Here's the thing, if you're doing the best you can with the information and tools you have at that moment, that's all that who can ask of you? That may be the secret to life. So give yourself some grace; you're doing great.

*I am doing great*
*I am doing great*

A place for the inkblot,

A place for the inkblot,

# 30 Days Of Affirmation

## Day 20

You know those urban stories where the mom is in a car accident, and her baby is trapped, so she grows some superhuman strength and flips the car off of her baby, saving its life? Yeah, that's real, and many unexplainable things like that have been exhaustively documented. But, I didn't know how strong I could be until I had no other choice. Now, I sincerely hope you don't need to find that out, but I suspect that inside your body are steel veins; if you need to, you'll turn into that superhero that can perform miracles. You are much stronger than you seem.

*I am stronger than I seem*

*I am stronger than I seem*

A place for the inkblot,

A place for the inkblot,

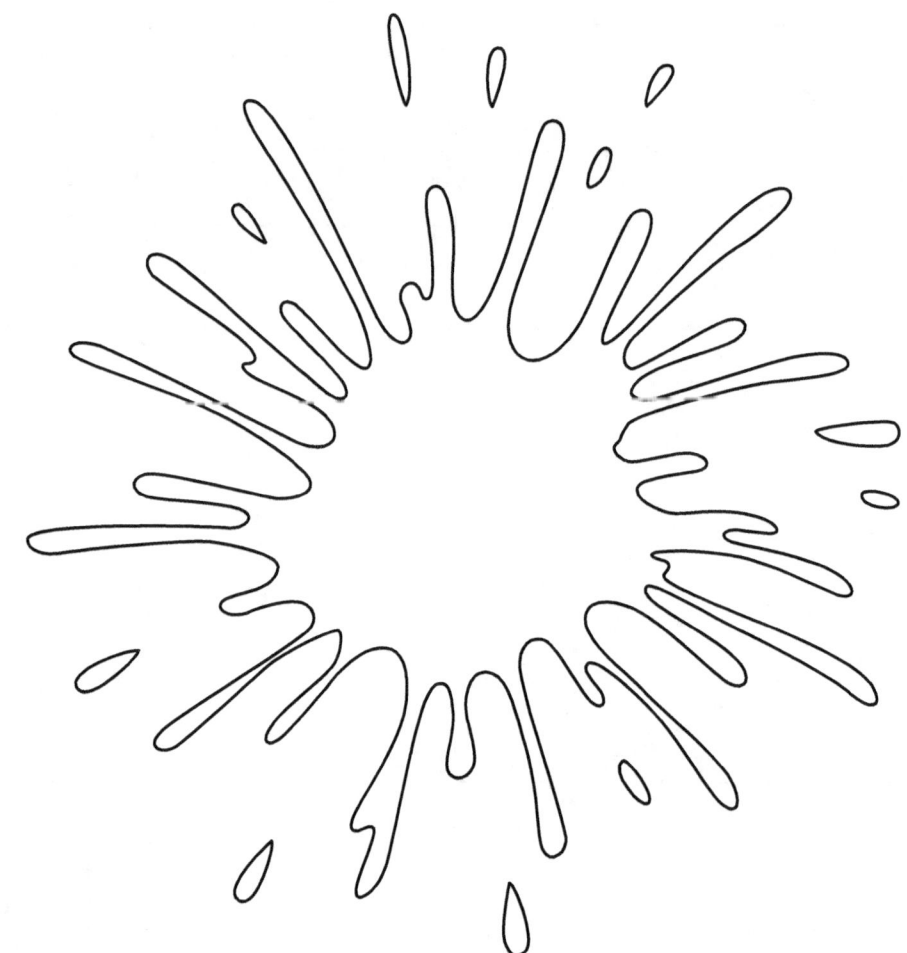

# 30 Days Of Affirmation

## Day 21

Bravery has this bad wrap. People think that to be brave, you need to run into burning buildings or perform some dramatic miracle, but I submit to you that that's not true. Being brave is trying again to be sober, even though you've already failed at it in the past. What's heroic is saying I love you for the first time. What's brave is being vulnerable with someone in your life and asking for help. What's heroic is falling and deciding it's still worth getting back up and trying again. And friend, it is so worth it. You are braver than even you believe.

*I am braver than I believe*

*I am braver than I believe*

*A place for the inkblot,*

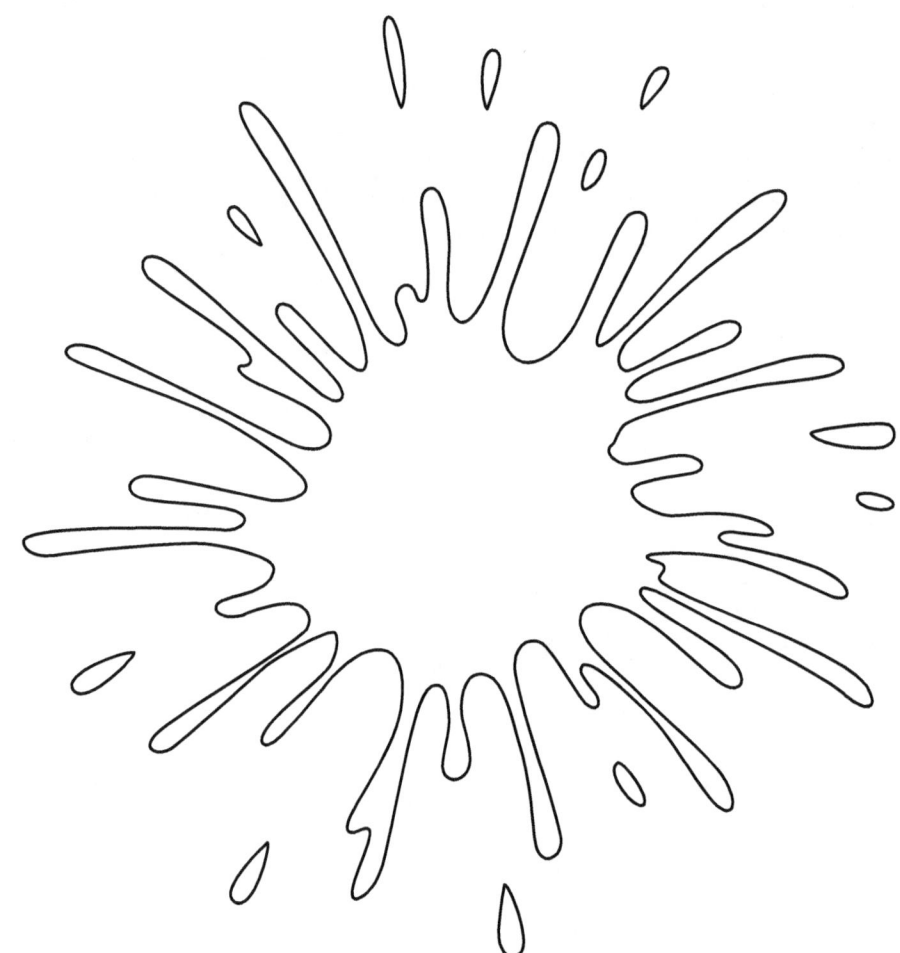

*A place for the inkblot,*

# Day 22

Too often, we second guess or doubt ourselves, our decisions, or our feelings. The truth is that we are all born with a Knowing and a Voice. The Knowing has no words. It is this feeling that we sometimes get. Maybe it's our soul, or perhaps it's just the part of our brain that lacks the capacity for words. We also have this Voice, and sometimes it sounds just like us, but that Voice in your head has a dirty little secret. It is a liar. Every time the Voice in your head says you aren't worthy, or you're too fat or too thin, or too much, it's lying to you. You are so wicked smart that with a little experience and practice, you can learn to tell the difference between the inner Knowing and the lies that the Voice is spewing in your head. You're smarter than you think.

*I am smarter than I think*

*I am smarter than I think*

*A place for the inkblot,*

*A place for the inkblot,*

# 30 Days Of Affirmation

## Day 23

There is a tiny safe place inside you where no one and nothing can get to you. Victor Frankel, a holocaust survivor, talks extensively about this, but to summarize quickly and poorly, there is a place inside of you that no one can take from you no matter how terrible things get on the outside. You can be tortured, beaten, starved, mentally abused, and just about anything else really, really awful and still find this small place inside yourself where you are safe. The odds are that what you're going through now is quite a bit less than all he went through, but know that there are resources for what you need, and you are safe now.

*I am safe*

*I am safe*

*A place for the inkblot,*

A place for the inkblot,

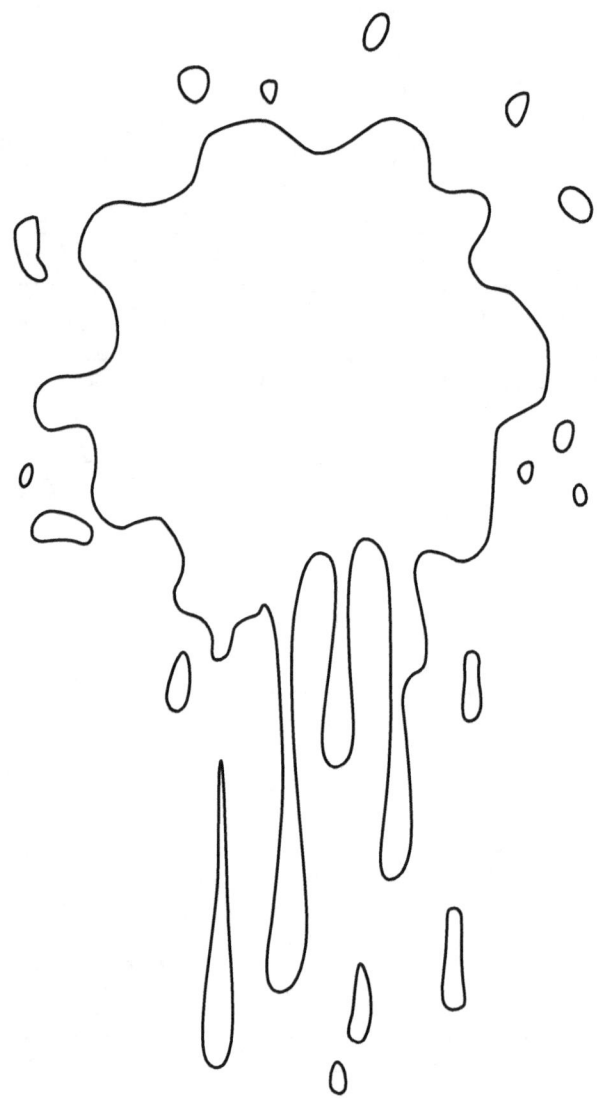

# 30 Days Of Affirmation
## Day 24

Anxiety can be a terrible monkey that we carry around on our backs. Lots of times, we try to rationalize or make deals with ourselves. It will be okay when my kids are out of diapers. It will be okay when I get this promotion at work. It will be okay when my partner finally acknowledges I'm right. I have news for you—some of those things may never happen, and the ones that do will produce happiness for five days or 5 minutes or 5 seconds, but it will never last. Train your brain to look at things as they are and to be grateful for things as they will be soon. It's already okay at this very moment.

*It is already okay*

*It is already okay*

A place for the inkblot,

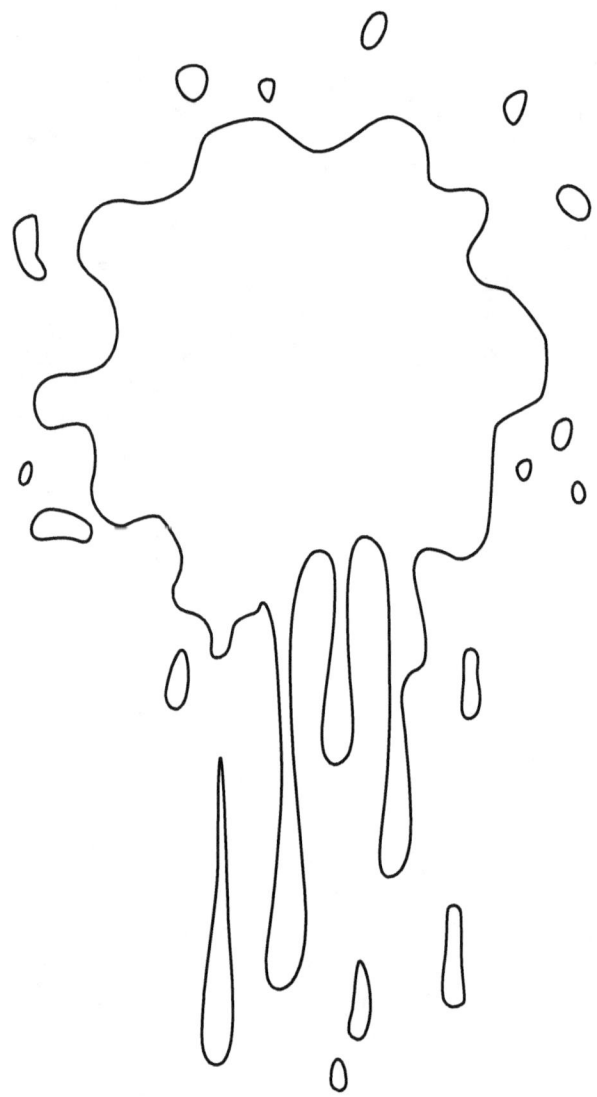

*A place for the inkblot,*

# 30 Days Of Affirmation

## Day 25

Peace can be a tricky thing. I know I have made my inner peace so conditional. I have woken up, done this fantastic morning routine, meditated, and done everything the gurus say you "should" do. Then get in my car to go to work, someone will cut me off, and suddenly I'm all road rage and driving like a pissed-off angry teenager. I realize that the hard-won peace I felt moments before was so cheap that I gave it away all in seconds for something that another person probably isn't even thinking Choosing peace in your heart, Your mind is a decision that is made repeatedly, hour by hour, and day by day. It really can make a big impact on your life. Start to notice when you're all worked up about something and realize that you can simply choose, at that moment, to experience peace.

*I choose peace*

*I choose peace*

*A place for the inkblot,*

*A place for the inkblot,*

# 30 Days Of Affirmation

## Day 26

Do you like to party? I do! Is a core value in our house and if all the other stuff we've been talking about is true, like what you focus on grows, then if you celebrate your wins, you get more wins to celebrate! Some days it's simply getting out of bed and brushing your teeth. Other days it is closing big deals, getting engaged, or getting a big promotion at work. There is nothing too small to celebrate-get to it!

*The more I celebrate the more I get to celebrate*

*A place for the inkblot,*

A place for the inkblot,

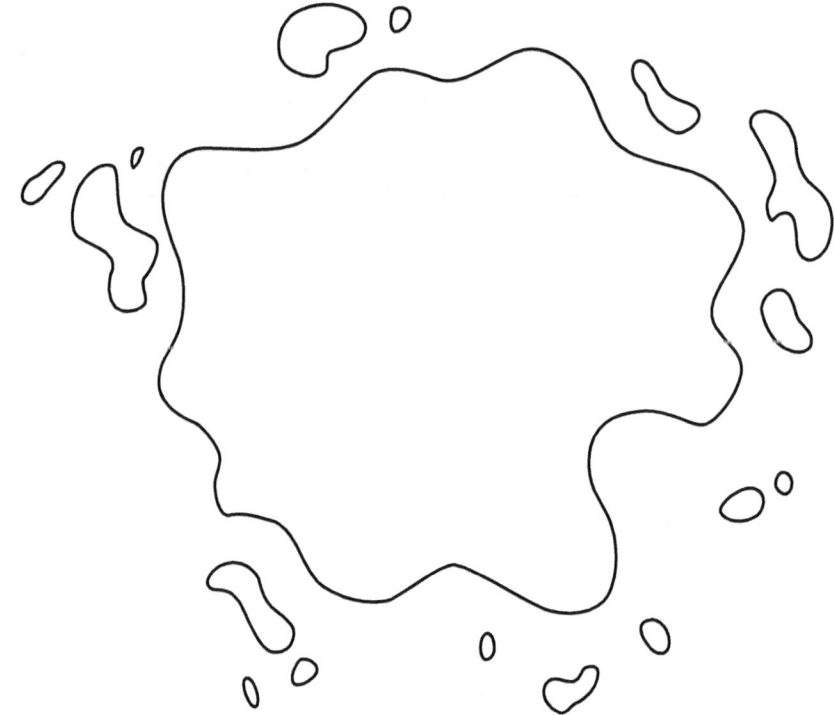

# 30 Days Of Affirmation

## Day 27

You, me, and everyone on the planet are born with this as their birthright. Therefore, you are worthy of giving and receiving love. There is nothing you need to do to become or prove that statement to be true. If you haven't heard it yet today, you are so loved.

*I am worthy of love*

*I am worthy of love*

A place for the inkblot,

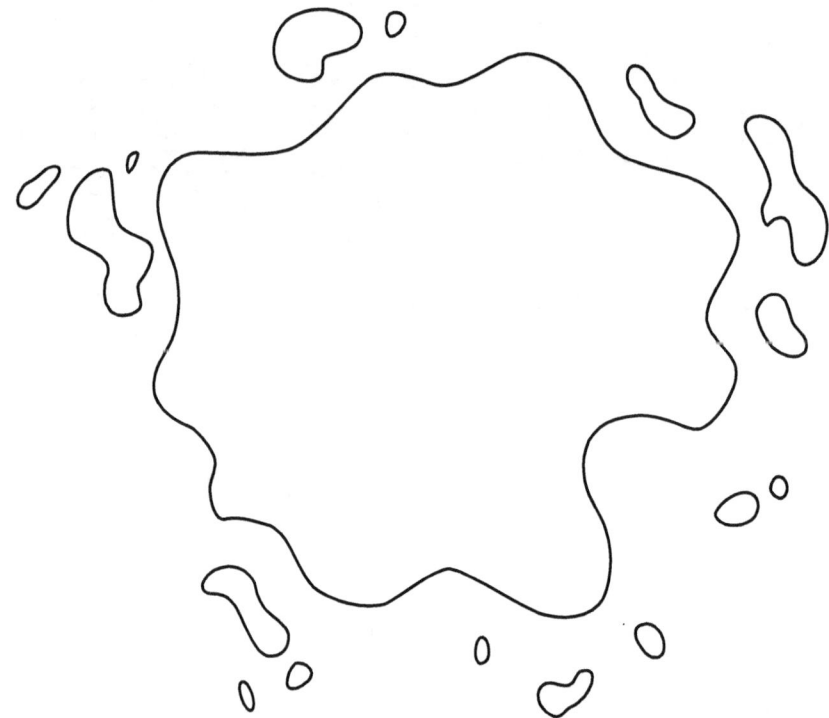

A place for the inkblot,

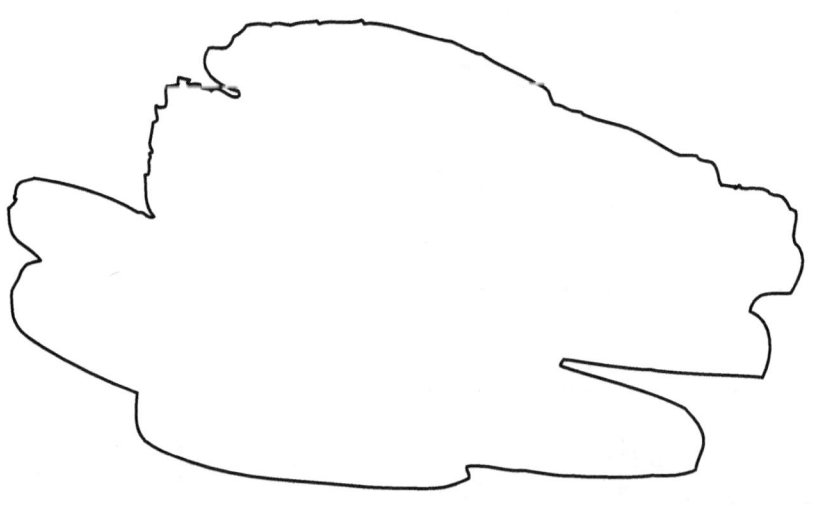

# 30 Days Of Affirmation

## Day 28

Ask anyone who has experienced a significant health scare or lost someone close to them that they love, and they will tell you—the present is a gift. Waking up in the morning is a gift. Growing old is a gift many deny, so if you start noticing wrinkles and grey hairs, congratulations. Celebrate that and realize that one more day on this planet is one more day you get the opportunity to love wholeheartedly. It's the opportunity to smile and brighten someone else's day. Today is one more day that you can change. Your life is a gift.

*My life is a gift*

*My life is a gift*

A place for the inkblot,

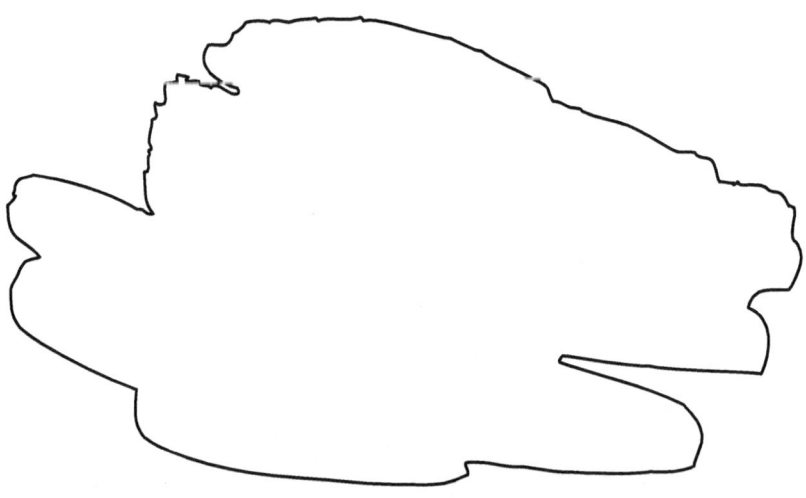

A place for the inkblot,

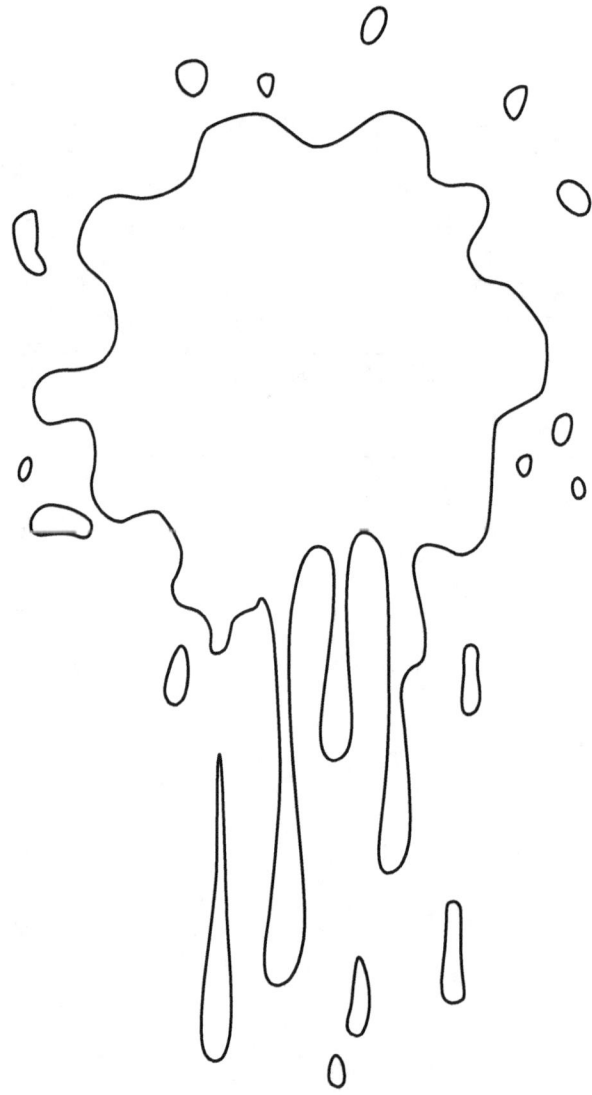

# 30 Days Of Affirmation

## Day 29

As a woman, I was taught from a young age to deflect receiving. Do you like this dress? Oh, this old thing? That's deflecting, and it's not healthy. Asking for help, receiving compliments, or even being able to receive feedback is a skill, just like painting nail polish on your toes. You can practice it and develop that talent. The secret is that the more you are open to receiving, the more good things find their way to you. Imagine going to the sea shore, and the ocean represents everything that you want, desire, and love in life. Do you want to show up with a teaspoon or a dump truck? The Universe will give you exactly what you ask for, so go ahead. Get that dump truck ready because your capacity to receive is growing infinitely every day.

*My capacity to receive is infinite*

*A place for the inkblot,*

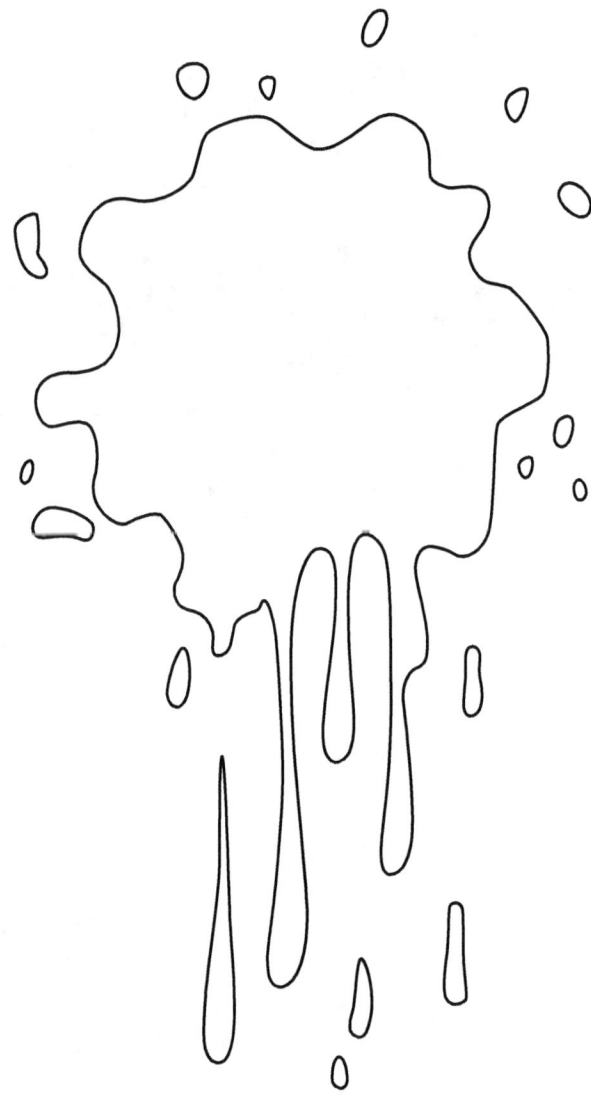

A place for the inkblot,

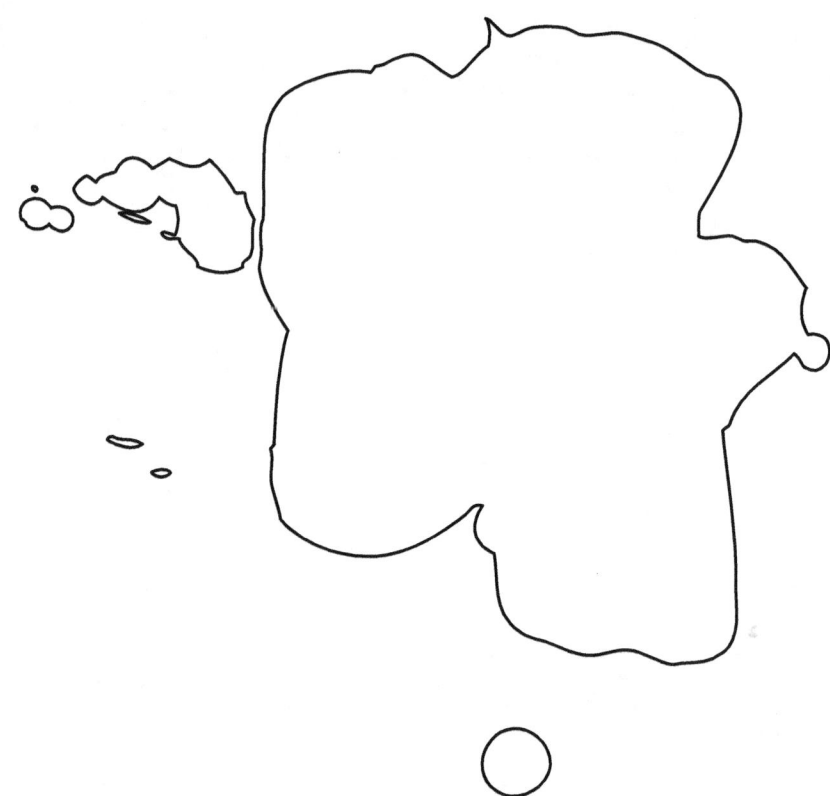

# 30 Days Of Affirmation

## Day 30

You know what to do next. Trust your inner self: honestly, do you want to learn a trick? Just pretend for a minute that there are no restrictions and limitations on your life. What would you do? Uh, huh. Well, guess what? There are no limitations or restrictions, so you just found your answer.

*I know exactly what to do next*

*A place for the inkblot,*

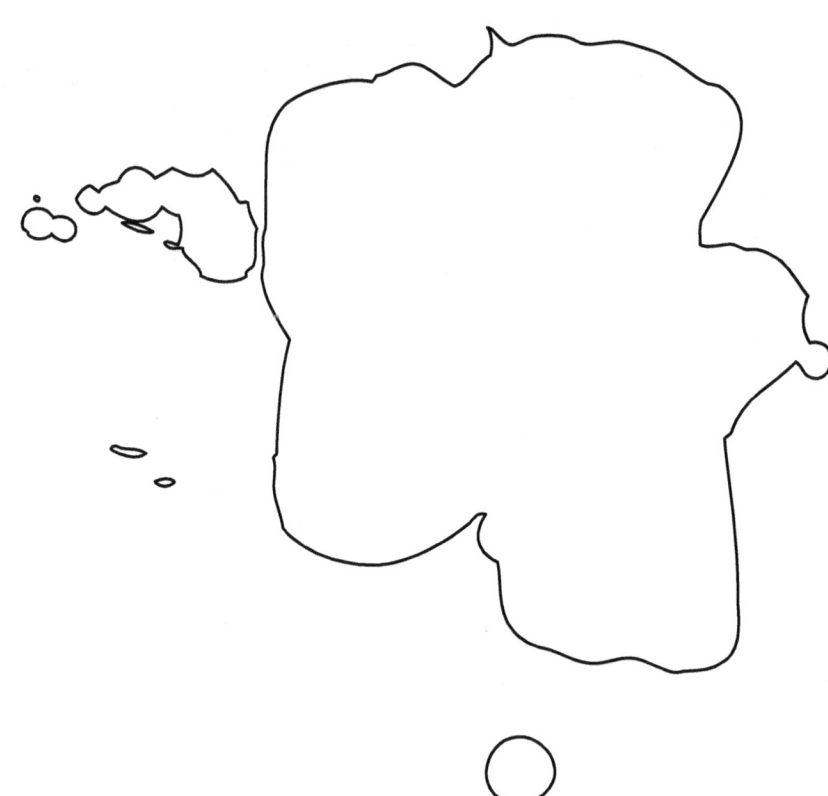

I want to thank you for purchasing this book. I would be very grateful for taking a moment and leaving feedback. It helps our small business grow and reach more people.